ANIMALS On the Move!

Animals That FLY

by Pearl Markovics

Consultant:
Beth Gambro
Reading Specialist
Yorkville, Illinois

Contents

Animals That Fly 2

Key Words 16

Index. 16

About the Author 16

BEARPORT
PUBLISHING

New York, New York

Animals That Fly

What can fly?

A bee can fly.

What can fly?

A duck can fly.

What can fly?

A bat can fly.

What can fly?

A dragonfly can fly.

What can fly?

An eagle can fly.

What can fly?

A butterfly can fly.

Can you fly?

Yes, you can!

Key Words

bat

bee

butterfly

dragonfly

duck

eagle

Index

bat 6–7
bee 2–3

butterfly 12–13
dragonfly 8–9

duck 4–5
eagle 10–11

About the Author

Pearl Markovics wishes she had wings and could soar across the sky. Don't you, too?

Teaching Tips

Before Reading
- ✔ Guide readers on a "picture walk" through the text by asking them to name the animals shown.
- ✔ Discuss book structure by showing children where text will appear consistently on pages.
- ✔ Highlight the supportive pattern, such as the question-and-answer format of the book. Note the consistent number of words found on each alternating page.

During Reading
- ✔ Encourage readers to "read with your finger" and point to each word as it is read. Stop periodically to ask children to point to a specific word in the text.
- ✔ Reading strategies: When encountering unknown words, prompt readers with encouraging cues such as:
    - **Does that word look like a word you already know?**
    - **It could be _____ , but look at _____ .**
    - **Check the picture.**

After Reading
- ✔ Write the key words on index cards.
    - **Have readers match them to pictures in the book.**
    - **Have children sort words by category (words that start with *b* or *d*, for example).**
- ✔ Encourage readers to talk about other animals that fly. Discuss different ways that animals move.
- ✔ Ask readers to identify their favorite page in the book. Have them read that page aloud.

Credits: Cover, © DMS Foto/Shutterstock; 1, © Butterfly Hunter/Shutterstock; 2–3, © Schnuddel/iStock; 4–5, © Steve Gettle/Minden Pictures; 6–7, © Chien Lee/Minden Pictures; 8–9, © Michael Durham/Minden Pictures; 10–11, © JT Fisherman/Shutterstock; 12–13, © dlamb302/Shutterstock; 14–15, © jekjob/Shutterstock and © KK Tan/Shutterstock; 16T (L to R), © Chien Lee/Minden Pictures, © Schnuddel/iStock, and © dlamb302/Shutterstock; 16B (L to R), © Michael Durham/Minden Pictures, © Steve Gettle/Minden Pictures, and © JT Fisherman/Shutterstock.

Publisher: Kenn Goin **Senior Editor:** Joyce Tavolacci **Creative Director:** Spencer Brinker

Library of Congress Cataloging-in-Publication Data Names: Markovics, Pearl, author. Title: Animals that fly / by Pearl Markovics. Description: New York, New York : Bearport Publishing, [2019] | Series: Animals on the move! | Includes bibliographical references and index. Identifiers: LCCN 2018014444 (print) | LCCN 2018020341 (ebook) | ISBN 9781642800258 (Ebook) | ISBN 9781642800036 (library) | ISBN 9781642801439 (pbk.) Subjects: LCSH: Animal flight—Juvenile literature. Classification: LCC QP310.F5 (ebook) | LCC QP310.F5 M37 2019 (print) | DDC 591.5/7—dc23 LC record available at https://lccn.loc.gov/2018014444

Copyright © 2019 Bearport Publishing Company, Inc. All rights reserved. No part of this publication may be reproduced in whole or in part, stored in any retrieval system, or transmitted in any form or by any means, electronic, mechanical, photocopying, recording, or otherwise, without written permission from the publisher. For more information, write to Bearport Publishing Company, Inc., 45 West 21 Street, Suite 3B, New York, New York, 10010. Printed in the United States of America.

10 9 8 7 6 5 4 3 2 1

CANCELLED
Westlake Porter Library
Westlake, OH 44145